Runes, The History, I
Use Them: A Magi
B

Written by
D. Brewer

Copyright

'Runes, The History, Meanings And How To Use Them: A
Magic Symbol Reference Book'

First published in August 2022 by D. Brewer
Printed & bound by Lulu Press
Distributed by Lulu Press

ISBN-13: 978-1-4710-9898-7

First Edition

Within This Book

- What Are Runes?
- Elder Futhark
- Anglo-Saxon (Anglo-Frisian) Futhorc
- Marcomannic
- Younger Futhark
- Hälsinge Runes (Staveless Runes)
- Medieval
- Dalecarlian
- Runic Magic & Divination
  - Bindrunes
  - Stacked Runes
  - The Kylver Stone
  - The Sjælland Bracteate
  - The Lindholm Amulet
  - The Kragehul Lance Shaft
  - Vadstena Bracteate
  - Undley Bracteate
  - The Seven Magic Anglo-Saxon Runic Rings
  - Runestones with Curses
- Medieval Rune Magic
  - Poetic Edda
  - Sigrdrífumál
  - Hávamál
  - Ynglinga Saga
  - Egil's Saga
- Modern Rune Magic
  - Alchemy
  - Adulruna
  - Armanen Futharkh
  - SS-Runen
  - The Present Day
  - Modern Day Rune Casting

Note

The author of this book does not dispense medical advice or prescribe the use of any technique as a form of treatment for physical, emotional or medical problems. The intent of the author is only to offer information of a general nature to help you in your search for emotional and spiritual well-being. In the event you use any of the information in this book for yourself, the author assumes no responsibility for your actions.

What Are Runes?

It is thought the word 'rune' is derived from the Proto-Germanic word 'rūnō', which means 'letter', 'literature' and 'secret' and also from the Germanic word 'run' and the Gothic 'runa', meaning 'secret' and 'whisper'. (Koch 2020).

Runes are defined as sets of symbols that make up alphabets, used initially by Germanic people of the Viking Age of central and northern Europe, probably inspired by the Latin alphabet of the Romans, to communicate in a written form. Runology is the study of runes and their history.

As well as a form of communication, each individual runic symbol is said to hold an inherent powerful magical nature and hence they have also been used for magic and divination, and examples are found over 2000 years of history regarding this type of use.

The earliest references to runic inscriptions appear from the end of the 1st century AD, and their use continued until Latin began to take over from the 11th century AD onwards due to Christianisation.

However, runic alphabets continued to evolve and be used for more specialised writings and magical influence and examples can be found right up until the present day.

Elder Futhark

Also known as Older Futhark, Old Futhark and Germanic Futhark, this set of 24 runes is said to be oldest, being in use from 2nd – 8th centuries AD.

It was used by the Germanic people and was inscribed on amulets, jewellery, pottery, tools and weapons. It was also carved in Scandinavian runestones, some of which can still be seen today, such as the Kylver Stone, found in a cemetery in Kylver, Stånga, Gotland, in 1903.

1.

ᚠ

- Name: Fehu
- Phonic sound: f or v
- Meaning: Sheep, cattle, wealth or money

2.

ᚢ

- Name: Ūruz or Ūra
- Phonic sound: u
- Meaning: Rain, water or slag

3.

þ

- Name: þurisaz
- Phonic sound: þ or th
- Meaning: Giant

4.

ᚨ

- Name: Ansuz

- Phonic sound: a

- Meaning: God or deity

5.

ᚱ

- Name: Raidiō

- Phonic sound: r

- Meaning: Journey or travel by horse

6.

〈

- Name: Kaunan, kauną or kenaz
- Phonic sound: k or c
- Meaning: Ulcer or torch

7.

ᚷ

- Name: Gebō
- Phonic sound: g
- Meaning: Gift

8.

ᚹ

- Name: Wunjō
- Phonic sound: w
- Meaning: Joy

9.

ᚺ   ᚺ

- Name: Hagalaz or Haglaz
- Phonic sound: h
- Meaning: Hail (the precipitation)

10.

ᚾ

- Name: Naudiz
- Phonic sound: n
- Meaning: Need and Distress

11.

ᛁ

- Name: īsaz
- Phonic sound: i
- Meaning: Ice

12.

- Name: Jēra
- Phonic sound: j
- Meaning: Good harvest and good year

13.

- Name: Eīwaz or Eïhaz
- Phonic sound: ï or æ
- Meaning: Yew tree or yew wood

14.

- Name: Perþ or Perþō
- Phonic sound: p
- Meaning: Pear tree, fruit tree or pear wood

15.

Y

- Name: Algiz or Elhaz
- Phonic sound: z
- Meaning: Elk, or protection or defence

16.

ᛊ ᛋ

- Name: Sōwilō
- Phonic sound: s
- Meaning: Sun

17.

↑

- Name: Tīwaz or Tēiwaz
- Phonic sound: t
- Meaning: Tiwaz (the god)

18.

ᛒ

- Name: Berkanan
- Phonic sound: b
- Meaning: Birch tree or birch wood

19.

ᛖ

- Name: Ehwaz
- Phonic sound: e
- Meaning: Horse

20.

ᛗ

- Name: Mannaz
- Phonic sound: m
- Meaning: Man

21.

ᛚ

- Name: Laguz or Laukaz
- Phonic sound: l
- Meaning: Water or lake

22.

◇ ◻

- Name: Ingwaz
- Phonic sound: ŋ
- Meaning: Ingwaz (the god)

23.

ᛟ

- Name: Ōþila, Ōþala, Ōþalan or Odal
- Phonic sound: o
- Meaning: Possession, estate or inheritance

24.

ᛞ

- Name: Dagaz
- Phonic sound: d
- Meaning: Day

Anglo-Saxon (Anglo-Frisian) Futhorc

These runes were known as the Futhorc. They were first used by the people of Frisia, a culture in North western Europe, and then by the Anglo Saxons of Britain, from the 5th century. They are also referred to as the Anglo-Frisian Futhawk.

The earliest known example of the use of these runes is found on the 5th century 'Undley Bracteate'; a gold medal-like piece of jewellery, found in Undley Common, near Lakenheath, Suffolk, in the UK.

As the Futhorc was a development from the Elder Futhark, some of the symbols are the same, but their names and meanings can alter. Hence they are included here for ease of reference.

1.

ᚠ

- Name: Feh or Feoh
- Phonic sound: f or v
- Meaning: Cattle or wealth

2.

ᚢ

- Name: Ur or Ūr
- Phonic sound: u
- Meaning: Aurochs (An extinct cattle species)

3

ᚦ

- Name: ðorn or þorn
- Phonic sound: þ or th
- Meaning: Thorn

4.

ᚩ

- Name: os or ōs
- Phonic sound: o
- Meaning: Heathen god or Mouth

5.

R

- Name: Rada or Rād
- Phonic sound: r
- Meaning: Travel by horse

6.

ᚲ

- Name: Cen or Cēn
- Phonic sound: c
- Meaning: Torch

7.

X

- Name: Geofu or Gyfu
- Phonic sound: g
- Meaning: Gift

8.

ᚹ

- Name: Wyn or Wynn
- Phonic sound: w
- Meaning: Mirth

9.

ᚺ

- Name: Hægil or Hægl
- Phonic sound: h
- Meaning: Hail (the precipitation)

10.

ᚾ

- Name: Næd or Nēod
- Phonic sound: n
- Meaning: Need and Plight

11.

|

- Name: is or īs
- Phonic sound: i
- Meaning: Ice

12.

☓   ♦

- Name: Gær or Gēar
- Phonic sound: j
- Meaning: Year

13.

∫

- Name: ih or īw
- Phonic sound: ï
- Meaning: Yew tree

14.

ᛈ

- Name: Peord or Peorð
- Phonic sound: p
- Meaning: Pear tree

15.

ᛉ

- Name: Ilcs or Eolh
- Phonic sound: x
- Meaning: Elk

16.

ᛋ

- Name: Sygil or Sigel
- Phonic sound: s
- Meaning: Sun

17.

↑

- Name: Ti or Tīw
- Phonic sound: t
- Meaning: Planet Mars or Tyr, the god.

18.

ᛒ

- Name: Berc or Beorc
- Phonic sound: b
- Meaning: Birch tree

19.

ᛗ

- Name: Eh
- Phonic sound: e
- Meaning: Steed

20.

ᛗ

- Name: Mon or Mann
- Phonic sound: m
- Meaning: Man

21.

ᛚ

- Name: Lagu
- Phonic sound: l
- Meaning: Lake

22.

ᛝ

- Name: Ing
- Phonic sound: ŋ
- Meaning: Freyr, the god

23.

ᛟ

- Name: Oedil or ēðel
- Phonic sound: œ
- Meaning: Inherited land or native country

24.

ᛞ

- Name: Dæg
- Phonic sound: d
- Meaning: Day

25.

ᚪ

- Name: ac or āc
- Phonic sound: a
- Meaning: Oak tree

26.

ᚫ

- Name: æsc
- Phonic sound: æ
- Meaning: Ash tree

27.

ᛠ

- Name: ear or ēar
- Phonic sound: ea
- Meaning: Grave soil

28.

ᚣ

- Name: yr or ȳr
- Phonic sound: y
- Meaning: Yewen bow

29.

- Name: Calc
- Phonic sound: k
- Meaning: Chalk or sandal

30.

- Name: Gar
- Phonic sound: ḡ
- Meaning: Spear

31.

- Name: Cweorð
- Phonic sound: q
- Meaning: Fire

32.

M

- Name: Stan
- Phonic sound: st
- Meaning: Stone

33.

- Name: Kalc
- Phonic sound: k
- Meaning: Chalice or offerings

Marcomannic

The Marcomannic runes were thought to be used during the 8th and 9th centuries AD and it is a mixture of Elder Futhark and Anglo-Saxon Futhorc.

These runes are recorded in a treatise known as 'De Inventione Litterarum', thought to be created by Rabanus Maurus Magnentius, who was a Frankish Benedictine monk, also known as Hrabanus, which was kept in manuscripts from the Carolingian age and found in the southern part of the Carolingian empire, now known as Bavaria. These manuscripts suggested the runes originated from the Macromanni, a Germanic race that existed during the time of the Roman Empire, in the area now known as Hungary. This led to the name, Macromannic runes.

However, it is since thought, that these runes were actually the creation of Carolingian scholars, with the intention of representing the letters of the Latin alphabet with runic equivalents.

As before, because they are a development of two previous runic alphabets, some of the symbols are the same, but their names and meanings often alter. Hence they are included here for ease of reference.

1.

- Name: Asch
- Phonic sound: a

2.

- Name: Birith
- Phonic sound: b

3.

- Name: Khen
- Phonic sound: ch

4.

- Name: Thorn
- Phonic sound: þ

5.

- Name: Eho
- Phonic sound: e

6.

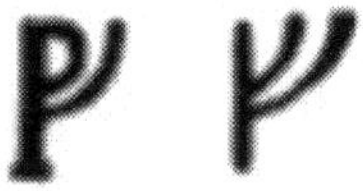

- Name: Fehc
- Phonic sound: f

7.

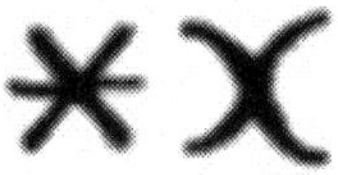

- Name: Gibu
- Phonic sound: g

8.

- Name: Hagale
- Phonic sound: h

9.

I

- Name: His
- Phonic sound: i

10.

ᚸᚾᚸ

- Name: Gilch
- Phonic sound: k

11.

ᛚ

- Name: Lagu
- Phonic sound: l

12.

ᛗ

- Name: Man
- Phonic sound: m

13.

- Name: Not
- Phonic sound: n

14.

- Name: Othil
- Phonic sound: o

15.

- Name: Perch
- Phonic sound: p

16.

- Name: Khon
- Phonic sound: q

17.

- Name: Rehit
- Phonic sound: r

18.

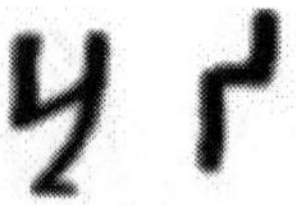

- Name: Suhil
- Phonic sound: s

19.

- Name: Tac
- Phonic sound: t

20.

- Name: Hur
- Phonic sound: u

21.

- Name: Helahe
- Phonic sound: x

22.

- Name: Huyri
- Phonic sound: y

23.

- Name: Ziu
- Phonic sound: z

Younger Futhark

The Younger Futhark are also known as the Scandinavian runes and Alphabet of the Norsemen. It is a reduced form of the Elder Futhark, used mainly in the 9th to 11th century.

The Younger Futhark runes can be further divided into two categories: 'long-branch' and 'short-twig. (Some symbols in each category are the same). Both can be found in Scandinavia, in Viking settlements.
Some say the long-branch runes were used by the Danes and the short-twig runes were used by the Swedish and Norwegians. Others say the difference between the two was purely functional, in that long-branch runes were used to mark stones, and short-twig runes were used in messages on wood.

1.

Long-branch   Short-twig

ᚠ   ᚠ

- Name: fé
- Phonic sound: f
- Meaning: Wealth

2.

Long-branch   Short-twig

ᚢ   ᚢ

- Name: úr
- Phonic sound: u
- Meaning: Iron / Rain

3.

Long-branch   Short-twig

ᚦ   ᚦ

- Name: Thurs
- Phonic sound: þ
- Meaning: thurs (a type of entity)

4.

Long-branch   Short-twig

ᚬ   ᚨ

- Name: As / Oss
- Phonic sound: ą
- Meaning: the god

5.

Long-branch   Short-twig

ᚱ   ᚱ

- Name: Reið
- Phonic sound: r
- Meaning: ride

6.

Long-branch   Short-twig

ᚲ   ᚲ

- Name: Kaun
- Phonic sound: k
- Meaning: ulcer

7.

Long-branch   Short-twig

᛬   ᛭

- Name: Hagall
- Phonic sound: h
- Meaning: Hail

8.

Long-branch   Short-twig

ᚾ   ᚿ

- Name: Nauðr
- Phonic sound: n
- Meaning: Need

9.

Long-branch   Short-twig

ᛁ   ᛁ

- Name: Ísa / Íss
- Phonic sound: i
- Meaning: Ice

10.

Long-branch   Short-twig

ᛅ   ᛆ

- Name: Ár
- Phonic sound: a
- Meaning: Plenty

11.

Long-branch   Short-twig

ᛋ   ᛁ

- Name: Sól
- Phonic sound: s
- Meaning: Sun

12.

Long-branch   Short-twig

ᛏ   ᛐ

- Name: Týr
- Phonic sound: t

- Meaning: Týr (the deity)

13.

Long-branch   Short-twig

ᛒ   ᛔ

- Name: Björk / Bjarkan / Bjarken
- Phonic sound: b

- Meaning: Birch

14.

Long-branch   Short-twig

Ψ   ↑

- Name: Maðr
- Phonic sound: m
- Meaning: Man / Human

15.

Long-branch   Short-twig

Γ   Γ

- Name: lögr
- Phonic sound: l
- Meaning: Sea

16.

Long-branch   Short-twig

⅄   I

- Name: Yr
- Phonic sound: R
- Meaning: Yew

Above: The 11th-century Ramsung Carving is a Swedish stone that uses the Younger Futhark runes to depict the legend of Sigurd, a Germanic hero who slayed a dragon and was later murdered.

Hälsinge Runes

The Hälsinge Runes, also known as the Staveless Runes, were a 10th century expansion of the Younger Futhark.

These runes appear different because they are written along one long stave.

The Högs Kyrka runestone in Hudiksvall, Sweden, is an example of a Viking monument with Staveless runic inscriptions.

Above: Högs Kyrka runestone. (Photograph by Håkan Svensson (2006))

Above: Hälsinge Runes

Medieval Runes

Medieval runes evolved in Scandinavia from the Younger Futhark, and provided a broader range of written language due to its greater inventory of symbols, enabling each symbol to be relating to just one specific sound, whereas the Younger Futhark, with only 16 symbols, was more restrictive.

It was used generally between the 12th and 15th centuries, and was fully developed by the 13th century, with mutual influences to and from the Latin alphabet.

In Iceland, medieval runes were still commonly used between the 16th and 18th centuries, and in Sweden, medieval runic calendars were used until the 19th century.

Medieval Rune Alphabet

ᛅᛒᛚᛐᚦᚦ
abcdþð

ᛐᛈᛈᛡᛁᛈ
efghik

ᚱᚤᚼᚻᛒᛈ
lmnopq

ᛋ ᚢᚨ
ᚱᛌᚾᚢᛈᛐ
rstuvy

ᛌᛐᛨ
zæø

44

Above: 16th century depiction of children being taught to use runic calendars (1555)
By Olaus Magnus (1490 – 1557)

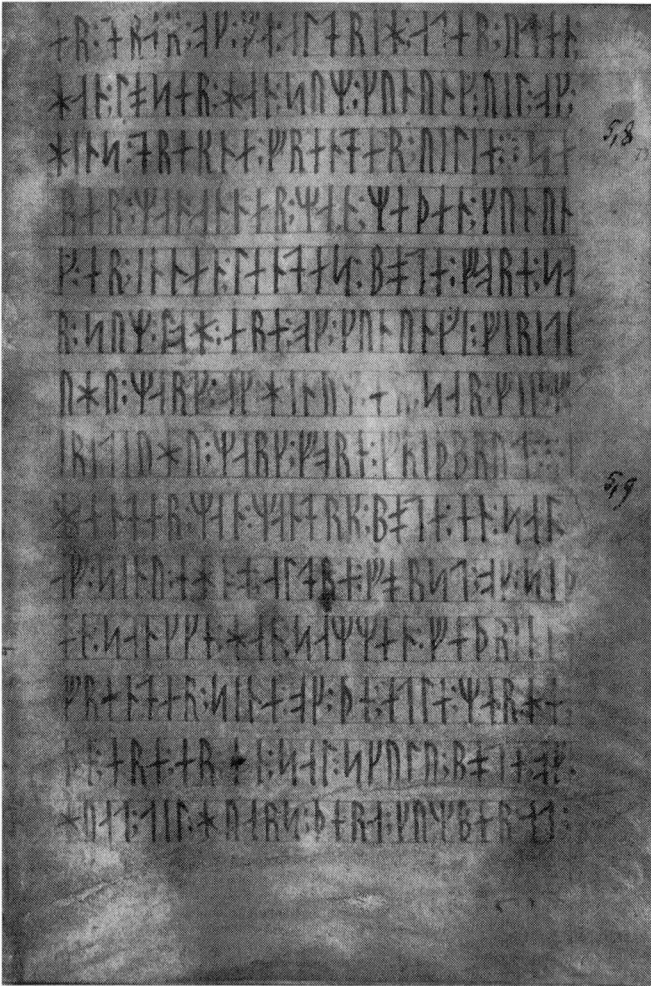

Above: Codex Runicus, a vellum manuscript from approximately 1300 AD containing one of the oldest and best preserved texts of the Scanian Law, written entirely in Medieval runes.

Above: A church bell from Saleby, Västergötland, in Sweden, containing a Medieval runic inscription from 1228 AD

Between the 16th and 20th centuries, in the province of Dalarna, Sweden, a mix of latin letters and runes evolved, becoming known as the Dalecarlian Runes. These were also known as the Dalrunes. The people of this area used this runic alphabet as marks of ownership on walls, stones, bowls, furniture, etc.

Dalecarlian Rune Alphabet

a b c d e f

g h i k l m

n o p r s t

u y å ä ö

Runic Magic And Divination

As well as being an early symbolic system of writing, runes also served a magic purpose. Many examples of their use for magic and supernatural purposes can be found through history.

In 98 AD, the Roman historian and politician, Publius Cornelius Tacitus (56 – 120 AD) gave an account of Germanic people using marks, thought to be runes to read omens:

"They attach the highest importance to the taking of auspices and casting lots. Their usual procedure with the lot is simple. They cut off a branch from a nut-bearing tree and slice it into strips these they mark with different signs and throw them at random onto a white cloth. Then the state's priest, if it is an official consultation, or the father of the family, in a private one, offers prayer to the gods and looking up towards heaven picks up three strips, one at a time, and, according to which sign they have previously been marked with, makes his interpretation. If the lots forbid an undertaking, there is no deliberation that day about the matter in question. If they allow it, further confirmation is required by taking auspices." (Birley, 1999).

Bindrunes

Bindrunes (also known as bind runes) are runes where two or more are combined together in one symbol.
For example:

The above symbol is a bindrune because it combines the Gebō 'X' and Ansuz 'ᚠ' of the Elder Futhark runic alphabet.

Inscriptions containing bindrunes are often thought to be of a magical nature.

Stacked Runes

Stacked runes, as the name suggests, are when individual runes are stacked into one symbol.
For example:

The above is a stacked rune because it is the Elder Futhark Tiwaz rune: ᛏ stacked upon itself.
As with bindrunes, the occurrence of stacked runes implies a magical inscription.

Sometimes a stacked rune may also contain a bindrune.

When a rune or set of runes are repeated consecutively, the inscription is also thought to be magical, such as a chant.

We will see examples of stacked runes, bindrunes, and repeated runes in magical inscriptions next.

The Kylver Stone

Another example of historical runic magic occurs on the Swedish Kylver Stone of 400 AD, which is inscribed with runes from the Elder Futhark alphabet. The end of the inscription contains a bindrune (or bind rune), made up of six stacked Tiwaz runes which was said to invoke the Norse god Tyr and four and four stacked Ansuz runes which invoked the gods of Æsir, the principle pantheon in Norse religion.

Interestingly, the Kilver Stone, found in 1903, was found covering a grave, and the runic inscription was face down, so it could not be read from the surface. Some speculate that the magic powers of the inscription were used to pacify the dead man.

Above: The Kylver Stone

ᚠᚾᛅᚱᛝᛁᚼᚼᛁᚾᚲᛋᛦᛦᛏᛨᛈᛈᛐᛚᛟᛞᚨᛦ

Above: The Runic Inscription

Above: The stacked bindrune that completes this inscription

The Sjælland Bracteate

The Sjælland bracteate is from Denmark, dated 500 AD, depicting a man's head above a four legged animal, possibly a horse. This is a common symbol representing the god Odin. The bracteate bears an Elder Futhark inscription which ends with a triple stacked Tiwaz rune to invoke the god Tyr.

Above: Copy of Sjælland bracteate

The inscription reads:

ᚺᚨᚱᛁᚾᚺᚨᚺᚨᛁᛏᛁᚲᚨ : ᚹᚨᚱᚨᚢᛁᛋᚨ : ᚷᛁᛒᚾᚨᚢᚨ : ᛏᛏᛏ *(stacked)*
hariuha haitika : farauisa : gibu auja : ttt

The inscription can be translated as, "Hariuha I am called: the dangerous knowledgeable one: I give chance". (Krause, W. 1971).
'Chance' is thought to also mean 'luck'.

The inscription contains three stacked Tiwaz runes which would have been used to invoke the god Tyr. This is a common theme in magical carvings.

Above: 3 stacked Tiwaz runes

The Lindholm Amulet

The Lindholm amulet is a piece of bone cut into the shape of a rib, and carved with Elder Futhark runic inscriptions. It was found in a peat bog in Skåne, in Sweden in 1840 and is dated around 300 AD.

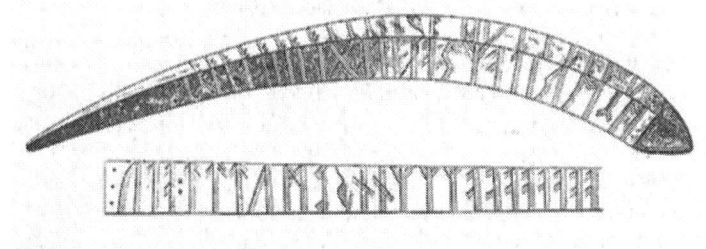

The two-lined inscription reads:

ᛗᚲᛗᚱᛁᛚᚠᛃᚼᚠ[ᛈ]ᛁᛚᚠᚷᚠᛃᚺᚠᛏᛗᚲᚨ:
ekerilazsa[w]ilagazhateka:

ᚠᚠᚠᚠᚠᚠᚠᚠᛃᛃᛃᚼᚼ[ᚾ]ᛒᛗᚢᛏᛏᛏ:ᚨᛚᚢ:
aaaaaaaazzznn[n]bmuttt:alu:

The first line has two possible translations: "I am called the wily" (as in crafty or deceitful) or "I am called Sawilagaz" (as in the one of the sun). This may refer to the god Odin.

The second line is thought to be a magical string of runes, in that it contains the three consecutive Tiwaz runes to invoke the god Tyr and eight consecutive Ansuz runes, to invoke the eight gods of Æsir. It also has three consecutive Algiz runes, which would have been used for protection and three consecutive Naudiz runes which ask for courage and wisdom against hardship and adversity.

ᛏᛏᛏ

Above: The 3 consecutive Tiwaz runes

ᚠᚠᚠᚠᚠᚠᚠᚠ

Above: The 8 consecutive Anzus runes

ᛉᛉᛉ

Above: The 3 consecutive Algiz runes

ᚾᚾ[ᚾ]

Above: The 3 consecutive Naudiz runes

Interestingly, the second line ends with the runic symbols Ansuz, Laguz and Uraz for 'alu'. This is an early runic charm word, often used carved on amulets and stones at the end of a magical string of runes or alone.

ᚠᛚᚢ

Above: The runic charm word, 'alu'

Also, the first line contains the word 'erilaz' which is found in several magical inscriptions, and is thought to mean 'magician' or 'rune master'. This refers to one who has the ability to use rune markings for magical purposes. However, this is contested, as some say it is some kind of military title or that it means 'noble warrior'. (Mees, 2003).

ᛗᚱᛁᛚᚨᛉ

Above: The runic word 'erilaz'

Kragehul Lance Shaft

The Kragehul Lance Shaft was also found in a peat bog, in Funen in Denmark in 1877 and it is from the 5th century AD.

Above: The Kragehul Lance Shaft.

The Elder Futhark inscription reads:

ek e=rila=z asugisalas m=uh=a h=aite g=ag=ag=a
ginu g=ah=e ... lija ... hagala wiju big–

Similar to the Lindholm amulet, we can clearly see the magical word 'erilaz'.

The first part of the inscription is interpreted as :
'I, the erilaz of Āsugīsalaz, am called Muha'.

The next part is interpreted as 'ga-ga-ga!' which is thought to be a ritual chant or battle cry.

The final part has several contested interpretations as follows:

1. A reference to a bull sacrifice;
"the mighty roarer [the sacrificial bull], the Hagal, I dedicate to the spear" (Schneider, 1969)

2. "magical-"ga", the helmet-destroying hail I dedicate to the spear" (Düwel, 1983)

3. "magical-god-gift, *(Odin)* hellish hail I dedicate upon this gift" (Peiper, 1999)

4. "I yell resoundingly, hail I dedicate in the s[pear]" (MacLeod, Mindy & Mees, 2006)

Vadstena Bracteate

The gold Vadstena Bracteate, found in 1774, in Vadstena, Sweden, dated 500 AD, like the Sjælland bracteate, depicts a man's head above a four legged animal, representing Odin. There is also a bird in front of the head.

Above: The Vadstena Bracteate

This bracteate contains the Elder Futhark runic inscription which reads:

tuwatuwa; fuþarkgw; hnijïpzs; tbemlŋod

This has not been interpreted, but the first part: 'tuwatuwa' is thought to be a magical chant because of its repetition.

Unfortunately, the bracteate was stolen from the Swedish Museum of National Antiquities in 1938 and has never been found.

Undley Bracteate

The 5th century AD Undley Bracteate was found in Undley Common, in Suffolk, UK. It depicts the image of the emperor Constantine the Great and the image of Romulus and Remus being suckled by the she-wolf.

Above: The Undley Bracteate

The inscription is written in Anglo-Frisian (Anglo-Saxon) Futhorc:

ᚷᚫᚷᚩᚷᚫ ᛗᚫᚷᚫ ᛗᛖᛞᚢ

Which reads:

g͡æg͡og͡æ mægæ medu

Notably, 'gægogæ' is inscribed as repeated bindrunes.

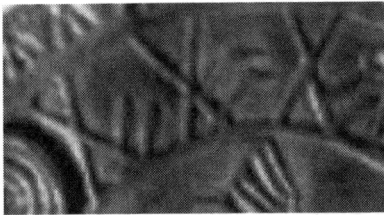

Above: The repeated bindrunes

Hence, the word 'gægogæ' is considered a magical chant within the inscription.

The Seven Magic Anglo-Saxon Rings

There are seven known Viking age Anglo-Saxon rings found in the UK from the 9th and 10th centuries that are inscribed with similar Anglo-Frisian (Anglo-Saxon) Futhorc Runes.
These are:

- Bramham Moor Ring
- Kingmoor Ring (Greymoor Hill Ring)
- Linstock Castle Ring
- Wheatley Hill Finger-Ring
- Coquet Island Ring
- Cramond Ring
- Thames Exchange Ring

These are each supposed to have a magical nature.

Bramham Moor Ring

This 9th century AD electrum (gold & niello) ring was found in West Yorkshire, UK.

(Photograph: Nationalmuseets Samlinger Online, 2017)

It's inscription is:

+ᚫᚱᛣᚱᛁᚢᚠᛚᛏ+ᛣᚱᛁᚢᚱᛁᚦᚩᚾ+ᚷᛚᚫᛋᛏᚫᛈᚩᚾᛏ͡ᚩᛚ

reading:
ærkriuflt | kriuriþon | glæstæpon͡tol

Notably, the n͡t is written as a bindrune: ᛏ͡ᚩ.

Kingmoor Ring (also known as the Greymoor Hill Ring)

This is a 9-10th century AD gold ring found near Carlisle, UK.

(Photograph: The British Museum, 2017)

The inscription is very similar to the Bramham Moor ring:

᛭ᚠᚱᛑᚱᛁᚢᚹᛁᛏᛑᚱᛁᚢᚱᛁᚦᚠ᛭ᚷᛚᚨᚹᛏᚠᛚᚨ᛭ / ᛏᚠᛚ

reading:
ærkriufltkriuriþonglæstæpon/tol

The last part, 'tol' or ᛏᚠᛚ is written on the inside of the ring.

Linstock Castle Ring

This is a 9th century AD red agate ring found near Linstock Castle, in Cumbria.

(Drawing: Stephens Handbook, 2015)

It's inscription is:

ᛗᚱᚪ•ᚱᛁ•ᚢᚹ•ᛞᚩᛚ•ᚪᚱᛁ•ᚦᚩᛚ•ᛚᛖᛋ•ᛏᛖ•ᚳᚩᛏᛖ•ᚾᚩᛚ•

reading:
ery.ri.uf.dol.yri.þol.les.te.pote.nol.

Again, we can see many similarities between this and the previous two ring's inscriptions.
It has been suggested that this ring may have been attached to the sword rather than worn on a finger, as it was found with swords in an Anglo-Saxon cemetery. (Dalton, 1912)

Wheatley Hill Finger-Ring

This is an 8th century AD gilded silver ring, found in County Durham. It has three settings, two of which are empty and the third contains red glass.

(Photograph: The British Museum, 2017)

It's inscription is:

[ᚻ]ᚱᛁᚾᚷᛁᚳᚻᚨᛏᛏ[ᚨ]

reading:

I am called ring

Coquet Island Ring

Now disintegrated into lead carbonate, this ring and its description is recorded in drawings by Stephens (1866) and Edward Charlton (1863).

a

b

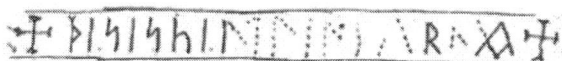

c

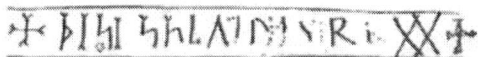

Cramond Ring

This leaded-bronze ring of the 9th – 10th century AD, was found in Cramond cemetery in Midlothian.

(Drawing: Stephens Handbook, 2015)

Much of the runic inscription is corroded away.

Thames Exchange Ring

This is a small copper alloy 10th century ring.

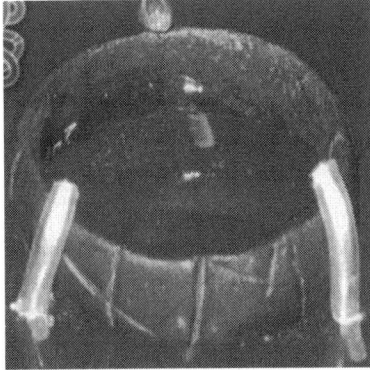

(Photograph: time.graphics)

The inscription reads:

ᛏfuþniine

This notably has two stacked Tiwaz runes, for invoking the god Tyr.

Ærkriu

Interestingly, in both the Bramham Moor ring and the Kingmoor ring, there is a phrase: 'ærkriu'. This phrase also appears in a 9th century AD Anglo-Saxon spellbook called 'Bald's Leechbook' (also known as 'Medicinale Anglicum') in a spell for staunching blood flow. With this in mind, the inscriptions are considered to be protection or healing charms, and the rings are therefore amulets.

Runestones with Curses

Runestone are raised stones or boulders upon which runic markings have been carved, mostly during the Viking Age (8th – 11th centuries AD), and most commonly found in Scandinavia. There are several stones with runic inscriptions that when interpreted contain curses that inflict harm on anyone who moves or breaks the stones:

- Stentoften Runestone
- Björketorp Runestone
- Skern Runestone
- Sønder Vinge stone 2
- Glavendrup stone
- Tryggevælde Runestone
- Glemminge stone
- Saleby Runestone

These rune stones are said to have a magical nature or power.

Stentoften Runestone

Discovered in Stentoften, Sweden, in 1823, this 7th century stone was found lying with the inscription face down, surrounded by five sharp stones, forming the shape of a pentagram. The runes that appear on this stone are a combination of Elder and Younger Futhark.

Above: The Stentoften Runestone

The English translation of the inscription on this stone reads:

(To the) dwellers (and) guests Haþuwulfar gave full year,
Hariwulfar ... ... I, master of the runes(?) conceal here nine
bucks, nine stallions, Haþuwulfar gave fruitful year,
Hariwulfar ... ... I, master of the runes(?) conceal here runes
of power. Incessantly (plagued by) maleficence, (doomed to)
insidious death (is) he who this breaks.
(Conradt, 2008)

Björketorp Runestone

The Björketorp Runestone was found in Blekinge, Sweden. Dated from the 6th or 7th century AD, this runestone is a 'menhir' (a man-made upright standing stone). It stands in a gravefield with other menhirs, some of which form stone circles and some which stand alone. Similar to the Stentoften Runestone, the runes that appear on this stone are a combination of Elder and Younger Futhark.
It is thought that the purpose of the curse written on this stone was to protect the graves.

The stone has two inscription on either side.

The shorter inscription translates to:
I prophesy destruction
or
I foresee perdition.

The longer inscription translates to:

I, master of the runes(?) conceal here runes of power.
Incessantly (plagued by) maleficence, (doomed to) insidious death (is) he who breaks this (monument).

Image: Montelius, O: Sveriges Hednatid (1877)

The Björketorp Runestone is the central stone in the image above.

A local legend exists around the Björketorp Runestone:

"When the stone was thought to be an impediment to the land, which a local man desired to cultivate, its removal was attempted. On a day of calm weather and with no winds, the local man piled wood around the stone, so he could heat the stone and then crack it by pouring cool water over the stone's surface. As the man set fire to the wood surrounding the stone, a gust of wind blew the flames away from the stone and towards the man, setting his hair on fire, and extinguishing the blaze around the Björketorp Runestone. The man, unable to quench the flames, died in terrible, flaming agony." (Jadewik, 2012)

The Skern Runestone is a 11th century Viking Age memorial stone found in Skjern, Denmark.
It depicts a carving of a face mask surrounded by a Younger Futhark runic inscription.

Above: Skern Runestone

The rune stone was found in the foundations of a staircase in the ruins of a 14th century castle in Skjern village. In those times, the significance of these inscribed stones was not understood and so they were often used in the construction of the foundations of buildings, walls, roads and bridges.

The inscription of this stone ends with a curse. It is translated as:

Sasgerðr, Finnulfr's daughter, raised the stone, in memory of Óðinkárr Ásbjǫrn's son, the valued and loyal to his lord.
A sorcerer (be) the man who breaks this monument!

Sønder Vinge Stone 2

The Sønder Vinge stone 2 is a granite stone, carved in the 10th century AD with Younger Futhark Runes. It was found to be a corner stone of Sønder Vinge Church in 1866 with its inscription facing outwards to be easily read.

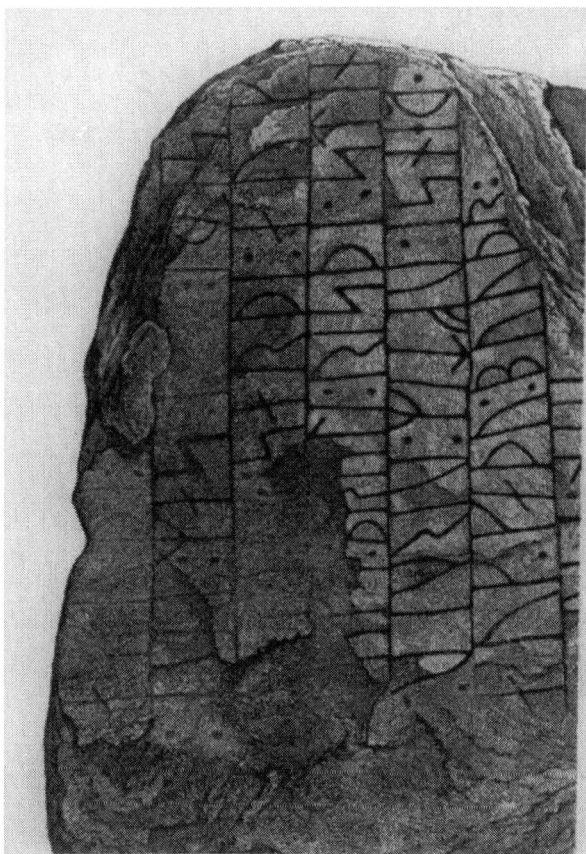

Photograph by Julius Magnus Petersen

This stone now resides in the porch of Sønder Vinge Church.

The inscription is partially eroded and so translation is somewhat patchy:

Guði <bi--li> raised this stone in memory of Órókia and Kaða, his two brothers ... wounded and bewitched(?). A warlock(?) (be) the man who destroys this memorial!

Auði Steward raised this stone in memory of Órókia and Kaða, his two brothers. [May he be considered] a pervert and a wizard(?), that man who destroys this memorial.

Glavendrup Stone

The Glavendrup Stone is an early 10th century runestone placed with other stones in the shape of a ship to mark a burial ground on the island of Funen in Denmark. Some of the other stones in the area are memorial stones with Latin inscriptions. This runestone completes the end of the stone ship.
The stone was discovered in a sand quarry in 1794
Every side of this upright stone is carved with rune markings, thought to be carved by the runemaster, Sote, and it is the longest runic inscription of any stone found in Denmark, with 210 characters.
When excavated, 9 graves were found at the eastern end of the stone ship, all empty.

The translation of the inscription is:

Ragnhildr placed this stone in memory of Alli the Pale, priest of the sanctuary, honourable þegn of the retinue.

Ragnhildr placed this stone in memory of Alli, priest of the Sølve, honourable þegn of the sanctuary-retinue.

Alli's sons made this monument in memory of their father, and his wife in memory of her husband. And Sóti carved these runes in memory of his lord. Þórr hallow these runes.

A warlock be he who damages(?) this stone or drags it (to stand) in memory of another.

Above: Drawing of Glavendrup Stone as part of the stone ship (1874)

Tryggevælde Runestone

Dated around 900 AD, the Tryggevælde Runestone was found on the island of Zealand, Denmark, on a barrow (burial mound).

Photograph by Christian Bickel

As with the Glavendrup Stone, this one is also thought to have been carved by the rune master, Sote.

Notably, this runestone also has circular holes cut into it, but no-one properly knows why. It has been suggested that they may have been made to aid transportation of the stone at some point in the past.

The inscription translates as:

Ragnhildr, Ulfr's sister, placed this stone and made this mound, and **this ship(-setting)**, in memory of her husband Gunnulfr, a clamorous man, Nerfir's son. Few will now be born better than him.

A warlock(?) be he who damages(?) this stone

or drags it (away) from here.

Glemminge Stone

Carved with Younger Futhark runes, this well preserved granite Viking Age stone is in a wall of Glimminge Church, in Scania, Sweden.

Photograph: Roberto Fortuna

The inscription translates as:

Sveini placed this stone in memory of Tosti the Sharp, his father, a very good husbandman. May whosoever breaks (it) become a warlock!

Saleby Runestone

Carved with Younger Futhark Runes, this Viking Age stone was found in the wall of Saleby Church, Sweden, and was subsequently moved to Dagsnäs Castle.

Above: Saleby Runestone

The Saleby Runestone is rare in that it is one of only a few raised in memory of a woman.

The inscription translates to

Freysteinn made these monuments in memory of Þóra, his wife. She was ... daughter, the best of her generation. May he who cuts to pieces ... breaks ... become a warlock and a maleficent woman ...

Medieval Rune Magic

There are several references to runes being involved in magic during medieval times in historical literacy.

Poetic Edda

One notable reference occurs in the Poetic Edda – a collection of anonymous poems from texts from the Icelandic manuscript called Codex Regius.

Sigrdrífumál

One particular section called Sigrdrífumál, (also known as Brynhildarljóð) relates to the meeting between the legendary Valkyrie Brynhild and the Germanic hero Sigurd.
Within this text, stanzas 5 – 12 involve runic magic.
In stanza 5, she brings Sigurd ale which she has charmed with runes:

> *"...Charms it holds and healing signs,*
> *Spells full good, and gladness-runes...."*

In stanza 6, she advises Sigurd to carve 'victory runes' on the hilt of his sword:

> *Victory runes you must know*
> *if you will have victory,*
> *and carve them on the sword's hilt,*
> *some on the grasp*

and some on the inlay,
and name Tyr twice.

Stanza 7 refers to *ølrunar* or Ale-runes – a spell to protect against being charmed by ale served by a host's wife.

Stanza 8 refers to *biargrunar* or birth-runes – a childbirth spell.

Stanza 9 refers to *brimrunar* or wave-runes – a spell to protect ships, where the runes must be carved on the mast and the rudder.

Stanza 10 refers to *limrunar* or branch-runes – a healing spell where the runes must be carved on eastward facing branches of trees.

Stanza 11 refers to *malrunar* or speech-runes – a spell to improve one's ability to vocalise their thoughts.

Stanza 12 refers to *hugrunar* or thought-runes – a spell to improve one's wit ability.

*Above: The title page of Olive Bray's English translation of
Codex Regius, Poetic Edda (1908)*

Above: The Valkyrie Brynhild (also known as Brünnhilde) by Richard Wagner, 1911

A Valkyrie is a female figure who guides the souls of deceased Nordic soldiers. She sends half of them to a place called Fólkvangor, a field ruled by the goddess Freyja, and the other half to Valhalla, a majestic hall in Asgard, ruled by the god Odin, where they become the 'einherjar', or 'army of one' for the Æsir (the principle pantheon gods). Here they are fed a beast called Sæhrímnir (thought to be a boar-like creature), who is slaughtered and cooked every night by the cook of the gods, Andhrimnir, and then brought back to life to be slaughtered and cooked again. The einherjar are also brought mead by the Valkyrie from the udder of the goat **Heiðrún**. This goat consumes foliage from the tree known both as **Læraðr** and **Yggdrasill**. Here, the einherjar prepare for the events of **Ragnarök**, a predicted series of battles and natural disasters, to take part in the future great battle in the field of **Vígríðr** between the Æsir gods and Surtr, the guard of the fiery realm, Múspell, who is predicted to engulf the Earth in fire and then the Earth will be reborn.

Above: Heiðrún consuming the foliage of Læraðr, by Lorenz Frølich (1895)

Hávamál

In another part of the Poetic Edda, is a poem entitled Hávamál, in which the god Odin quests for the runes.

The three Norns, (female entities of past, present and future, named Urd, Verdandi, and Skuld) carve the destiny of every person into the ancient bark at the base of the World-tree Yggdrasil using runes. Odin performs a self-sacrifice by using his own spear to impale himself on the tree. He fasts and stares into the Well of Urd. After hanging there for nine days and nights, Odin reaches out and finds the runes he quested within the tree and learns their true significance, secrets and magic.

*...I peered right down in the deep;
crying aloud I lifted the Runes...*

...Hidden Runes shalt thou seek and interpreted signs, many symbols of might and power...

In the poem, Odin is said to find eighteen songs (spells) in total which relate to runes.

Song one is a spell to calm the mind when it is troubled:

The first is Help which will bring thee help in all woes and in sorrow and strife.

Song two is a spell to relieve pain and heal injury:

A second I know, which the son of men must sing, who would heal the sick.

Song three is a spell to blunt the swords of enemies so that they cannot inflict harm:

A third I know: if sore need should come of a spell to stay my foes; when I sing that song, which shall blunt their swords, nor their weapons nor staves can wound.

Song four is a spell to enable escape from any method of binding:

A fourth I know: if men make fast in chains the joints of my limbs, when I sing that song which shall set me free, spring the fetters from hands and feet.

Song five is a spell to catch, stop or change the course of an arrow in flight:

A fifth I know: when I see, by foes shot, speeding a shaft through the host, flies it never so strongly I still can stay it, if I get but a glimpse of its flight.

Song six is a spell to turn any spell cast by an enemy, back to that enemy:

A sixth I know: when some thane would harm me in runes on a moist tree's root, on his head alone shall light the ills of the curse that he called upon mine.

Song seven is a chant to put out fires:

A seventh I know: if I see a hall high o'er the bench-mates blazing, flame it ne'er so fiercely I still can save it, --I know how to sing that song.

Song eight is a spell to calm anger and hatred:

An eighth I know: which all can sing for their weal if they learn it well; where hate shall wax 'mid the warrior sons, I can calm it soon with that song.

Song nine is a spell to calm a stormy sea:

A ninth I know: when need befalls me to save my vessel afloat, I hush the wind on the stormy wave, and soothe all the sea to rest.

Song ten is a chant to curse witches, shapeshifters and banish ghosts:

A tenth I know: when at night the witches ride and sport in the air, such spells I weave that they wander home out of skins and wits bewildered.

Song eleven is a blessing to protect soldiers and ensure them victory:

An eleventh I know: if haply I lead my old comrades out to war, I sing 'neath the shields, and they fare forth mightily safe into battle, safe out of battle, and safe return from the strife.

Song twelve is a spell to raise and speak with the dead:

A twelfth I know: if I see in a tree a corpse from a halter hanging, such spells I write, and paint in runes, that the being descends and speaks.

Song thirteen is a blessing whereby water is sprinkled on a child by the god Odin to protect them in battle:

A thirteenth I know: if the new-born son of a warrior I sprinkle with water, that youth will not fail when he fares to war, never slain shall he bow before sword.

Song fourteen is a gift of the knowledge of the nature any powerful entity:

A fourteenth I know: if I needs must number the Powers to the people of men, I know all the nature of gods and of elves which none can know untaught.

Song fifteen is a chant for wisdom, first uttered by the dwarf, Thjodrerir:

A fifteenth I know, which Folk-stirrer sang, the dwarf, at the gates of Dawn; he sang strength to the gods, and skill to the elves, and wisdom to Odin who utters.

Song sixteen is a love spell to arouse desire:

A sixteenth I know: when all sweetness and love I would win from some artful wench, her heart I turn, and the whole mind change of that fair-armed lady I love.

Song seventeen is a spell to make shy love be everlasting:

A seventeenth I know: so that e'en the shy maiden is slow to shun my love.

Song eighteen is a secret that Odin does not reveal:

An eighteenth I know: which I ne'er shall tell to maiden or wife of man save alone to my sister, or haply to her who folds me fast in her arms; most safe are secrets known to but one

Above: Odin, der Göttervater, by Wilhelm Wägner (1882)

Ynglinga Saga

In chapter 38 of the Icelandic poem Ynglinga Saga, written in 1225 AD by Snorri Sturluson, there is a section, referring to King Granmar of Södermanland (a Swedish province), which says:

...There, the chips fell in a way that said that he would not live long...

It is assumed that the 'chips' refer to runes that were being used predict the future.

Above: illustration from Ynglinga Saga 1225)

Egil's Saga

Written originally in 1243 AD, Egil's Saga revolves around four generations of the clan of Egill Skallagrimsson, an Icelandic Viking farmer and skaid (poet).

In one scene of this piece of literature, Egill is given a poisonous drink. Realising it is poisoned, he cuts runes on the drinking horn of the vessel and then cuts his hand, and paints the runes with his blood, thus rendering the drink harmless.

Painting runes in blood appears to be a common feature in medieval literature, suggesting it may have been a regular feature in the practice of runic magic.

Above: Portrait of Egill Skallagrimsson from a 17th century manuscript.

For reference, we are using the term 'modern' to cover runic use from the 17th century to the present day, as it was in the 17th century that the use of runes evolved further.

Alchemy

The purposes of alchemy were many and varied. Generally, alchemists were concerned with attaining the ability to mature, purify and perfect substances, and to allow the human state to attain perfection. (Powell, 1977). With this in mind, there were four main aims:

- The transmutation of common and inexpensive base metals such as lead into more precious noble metals such as, and most usually, gold.
- The creation of an 'elixir of immortality' which could grant eternal life or eternal youth.
- The creation of a 'panacea', a remedy that could universally cure all diseases and prolong life indefinitely.
- The creation of an 'alkahest', a universal solvent capable of dissolving every other substance, including gold.

To discover a mystical substance that could achieve these four mains aims of alchemy was the ultimate goal of alchemists, and this mythical substance was called the 'Philosopher's Stone'.

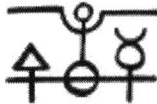

In 1403, the practice of alchemy, in part, was banned in England by King Henry IV. (Levin, 2010). In that same century, using symbols of alchemy and runes became considered heresy by the churches, and punishable by death. Hence, alchemists further encrypted their work using more elaborate secret coded symbols, to hide their illegal occupation and inevitably, some of the symbols were adopted from the rune systems.

While runic magic was being already practiced since much earlier times, the continuing secret alchemy work was now becoming shrouded in superstition and it inevitably became entangled with witchcraft and magic with the use of symbols of power.

Adulruna

In 1599, a civil servant in Stockholm named Johan Bure (1568-1652) also known as Johannes Bureus, took a particular interest in interpreting runestones. He began a trip across Sweden, visiting runestones to officially document, translate and interpret them.

Influenced by the practice of alchemy and the growing Rosicrucian movement of the time, (a movement professing esoteric and occult emphasis on mysticism and spiritual enlightenment), he became convinced of an occult nature in runic symbols, and drawing on elements of the Younger Futhark alphabet he developed a system of fifteen runes which he called the Adul Runes (Noble Runes).

Some of the runes hold more than one meaning and sound.

The Adul Runes

1.

ᛈ

- Name: Frey
- Phonic sound: f, v
- Meaning: Seeds, frog, cow, phallic fertility god.

2.

ꓘ

- Name: Ur
- Phonic sound: u, y
- Meaning: from, out of, clock, time.

3.

þ

- Name: Tors / Thors
- Phonic sound: t, th
- Meaning: to dare, God united, Thurs/Thor the god.

4.

ᚼ

- Name: Odhes / Odhen
- Phonic sound: o, a
- Meaning: Odin the god, oath, Mercury.

5.

ᚱ

- Name: Rydhur
- Phonic sound: r
- Meaning: advice, ride, rudder.

6.

ᚤ

- Name: Kyn
- Phonic sound: c, g, q
- Meaning: the nature of power.

7.

ᚼ

- Name: Haghall
- Phonic sound: h, gh, ch
- Meaning: skill, cunning, finesse, art, noble.

8.

- Name: Nadh
- Phonic sound: n
- Meaning: grace, distress.

9.

- Name: Idher
- Phonic sound: I, j
- Meaning: naked, remorse, repentance.

10.

- Name: Æru
- Phonic sound: æ, a
- Meaning: honour, eagle

11.

ᛣ

- Name: Sun
- Phonic sound: s, ss
- Meaning: highest sun, hanging sun, son of light

12.

ᛏ

- Name: Tidhr
- Phonic sound: t, d
- Meaning: tiger, priest

13.

ᛒ

- Name: Byrghal
- Phonic sound: b, p
- Meaning: start, gate, the microcosm, the spirit immersed In matter, son of war.

14.

ᛚ

- Name: Lagher
- Phonic sound: l, ll
- Meaning: drip, pour, bath, arrange, law.

15.

ᛘ

- Name: Man
- Phonic sound: m, mm
- Meaning: one who closes their mouth, man as the measure of everything.

Convinced of the magical nature of these runes, Johannes Bureus believed that their arrangement affected their powers and he experimented with arranging them in rows, on three faces of a cube, and in cross shapes.

ᛆ D ᚢ L Rᚢ N Æ

1 ᛈ   ᛈ   1
2 ᚼ   ᛲ   ↑
3 ᚦ   ᛏ   ᛒ
4 ᚼ   ᛁ   ᚱ
5 ᚿ   ✝   ᛦ

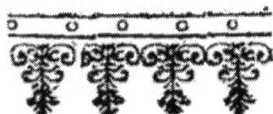

Above: The Rune Row

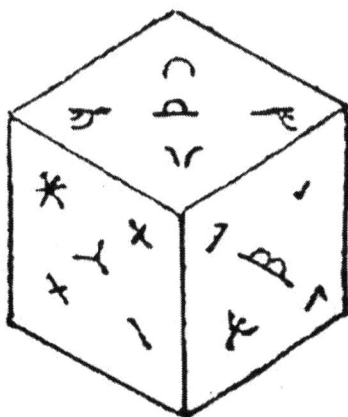

*Above, the cube arrangement was called the 'Falling Stone'.
On each side, the runes are arranged in a cross shape with
some of them mirror imaging each other.*

115

A DVL-RVNÆ
TITVLVS III
De Pastoris Sacerdotio.

Above: Adul Runes in a cross arrangement.

Johannes Bureus' cross arrangements included mirror imaging the symbols. It was thought that they were related to the Kabbalistic Tree of Life or the Yggdrasil World Tree.

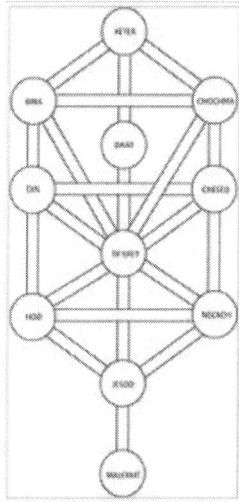

Above: Kabbalistic Tree of Life

Above: Yggdrasil World Tree

Bureus' cross arrangement represented the universe, the human, and the divine, with the vertical stem of the cross being the route to divinity.

To further his explanations of the cross, Bureus made further smaller crosses.

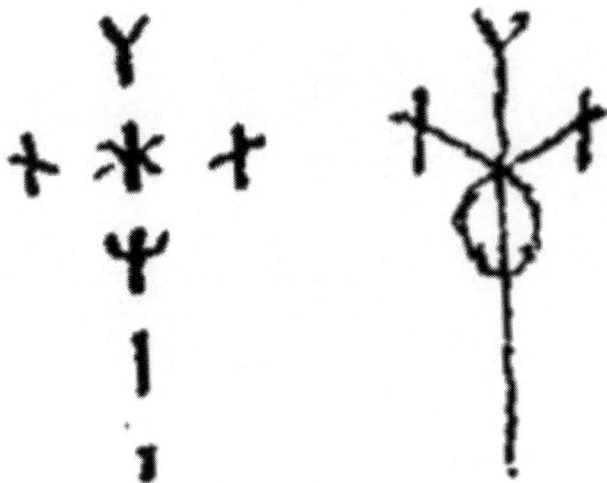

From the cross above on the left, he merged the symbols to make the cross above on the right.

In 1616, Johannes Bureus went on to write an early Rosicrucian script called 'Ara Foederis Theraphici F.X.R. Der Assertion Fraternitatis R.C....' In the illustration from the book below, we can clearly see the cross symbol that he developed earlier, above the alter.

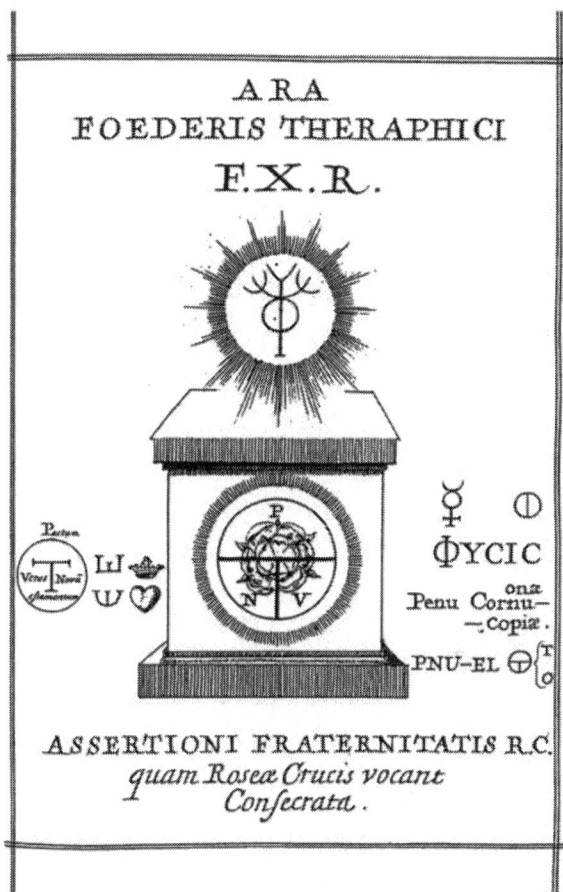

Above: Johannes Bureus

Armanen

In 1902, journalist, playwright and novelist Guido Karl Anton List (1848 – 1919) suffered 11 months of blindness and it was during this time that his interest in occultism grew and that he developed the Armanen Runes. He said that his blindness allowed his inner eye to open so that the Secret of the Runes was revealed to him.

List claimed that the inspiration came from the Hávamál in the Poetic Edda and Odin's quest for the runes. He said that the Secret of the Runes was encrypted in the eighteen Songs (spells) that Odin found. He called these, the 'Song of the 18 Runes'. He believed these to be the historic 'primal runes'.

The resulting symbols of the Armanen Futharkh were drawn from the Younger Futhark and the Anglo-Saxon Futhorc.

Armanen Futharkh

1.

- Name: Fa
- Phonic sound: f

2.

ᚢ

- Name: Ur
- Phonic sound: u

3.

ᚦ

- Name: Thurs
- Phonic sound: th / þ

4.

ᚫ

- Name: Os
- Phonic sound: a, o

5.

ᚱ

- Name: Rit
- Phonic sound: r

6.

Ɣ

- Name: Ka
- Phonic sound: k

7.

✳

- Name: Hagal / Hag
- Phonic sound: h
  List considered this to be the 'mother rune'

8.

↑

- Name: Nauth / Not
- Phonic sound: n

9.

|

- Name: Is
- Phonic sound: i

10.

- Name: Ar
- Phonic sound: a

11.

- Name: Sig / Sol
- Phonic sound: s

12.

- Name: Tyr
- Phonic sound: t
-

13.

- Name: Bar
- Phonic sound: b

14.

ᛚ

- Name: Laf
- Phonic sound: l

15.

ᛉ

- Name: Man
- Phonic sound: m

16.

ᛦ

- Name: Yr
- Phonic sound: y

17.

ᛇ

- Name: Eh
- Phonic sound: e

18.

- Name: Gibor / Ge /Gi
- Phonic sound: g

List published his Armanen Futharkh in a book titled Das Geheimnis der Runen in 1908 in Leipzig and Vienna. List's Armanen runic symbols were used significantly by the German ethno-nationalist Völkisch movement and then later in the Nazi movement.

Above: Circular Arrangement

Guido Karl Anton List (1848 – 1919)
Photograph taken in 1878

SS-Runen

Senior figures such as Himmler, during the few years before and during World War 2 believed the mystical qualities of these symbols could advance their cause and so they developed nine of the Armanen runes further to what was to become known as the SS-Runen (SS Runes) or the runic insignia of the Schutzstaffel. These symbols were displayed on flags and uniforms and other Nazi items and represented the ideals of the SS. Indeed, some of the SS were given lessons in runology to further understand the significance of these symbols.

SS-Runen

1.

- Name: Siegrune (Sig, Double Sig)

- Meaning: Victory

This symbol was adapted to become an emblem of the SS, notably because of its shape. It is still used in the neo-nazi movement and considered a symbol of hate among many.

Above: The SS emblem

2.

- Name: Eif

- Meaning: Zeal / Enthusiasm

This was used during the early development of the SS by close personnel to Hitler.

3.

- Name: Ger

- Meaning: Communal spirit

Communal spirit among their own was an ideal of the SS.

4.

- Name: Hagal

- Meaning: Faith in Nazism

Himmler considered this to signify unshakeable faith in Nazi ideology.

5.

- Name: Leben
- Meaning: Life

This emblem was widely seen on Nazi paramilitary uniforms and was also used as a symbol for birth.

6.

- Name: Odal
- Meaning: Kinsip, family, blood unity

This symbolised maintaining the racial purity of the SS.

7.

- Name: Opfer
- Meaning: Sacrifice

This was used to commemorate Nazi party members who had fallen during Hitler's failed coup d'etat in 1923, known as the Beer Hall Putsch or Munich Putsch.

8.

- Name: Tod

- Meaning: Death

The SS used this symbol to represent death on documents and grave markers.

9.

- Name: Tyr

- Meaning: Leadership in battle

Considered the battle rune, this was placed on SS graves. It was also used on the uniform of the Reichsführerschule who were responsible for training the SS until 1934.

The Nazis added three further symbols to complete the SS-Runen.

1.

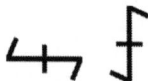

- Name: Wolfsangel

- Meaning: Liberty and Independence

Already used since the 15th century by a peasant's uprising, this was adopted by the SS and is still an apparent symbol in the municipal arms of many German towns.

2.

- Name: Heilszeichen

- Meaning: Prosperity

The SS used this symbol to represent good fortune and success. Interestingly, this is an adaptation of List's Gibor 'g' rune and a bindrune for List's 'o' and Tyr 't' rune.

3.

- Name: Swastika

This was originally an ancient religious symbol. The Nazis adopted it to represent the obsolete Aryan race, thought to be a (now disproven) supreme race of Proto-Indo-European heritage. This symbol became widely synonymous with the Nazi party and antisemitism and is now banned in many countries.

SS Death's Head Ring (SS-Ehrenring)

Also known as the SS Honour Ring or Skull Ring, this silver ring was an award given by Himmler to members of the SS. It had a Totenkopf skull and five runes (one repeated) etched on the outside and with Himmler's signature, award date and recipients name in the inside.

Above: an SS-Ehrenring

The SS Runes on this ring are etched in specific triangle, hexagonal, square and circle shapes:

'SIG' RUNE   'HAGAL' RUNE   'SWASTIKA' RUNE   'DOUBLE' RUNE

Between the runes are carved oak leaves. The oak tree was considered to have an important strong magical nature by ancient druids.

Himmler ordered that if an SS member was dismissed, retired or died, his ring was to be returned. They were stored in a chest at Wewelsburg Castle, in Büren, Germany, until towards the end of the war when Himmler ordered that they be blast sealed in Wewelsburg Hill and no more were to be made. Only a few of these rings still exist today and the whereabouts of many are unknown.

The Present Day

Since the latter part of the 20th century, interest in the magical nature of runology has grown, mainly to help answer life's questions.

Whereas the old name of one who could read the runes was an 'erilaz', now the reader is called a 'rune caster'.

The Elder Futhark has become increasingly popular with rune casting, possibly because it is the oldest of the runic alphabets and therefore holds more integrity having been the least altered. It remains the original runes. Many Elder Futhark sets now include a blank rune. This has two motivations. One is to replace a rune if it is lost. However, it has been suggested that the blank rune is the rune appertaining to the god Odin, representing the beginning and ending and "the divine in all human transactions". (Blum, 1987)

Modern runes are made in many different materials, including wood, stone, crystal, bone and metal and the methods of rune casting vary. A rune cloth is often used on which to place the runes. This is usually square and of natural cotton or linen and is white in colour.

In the next chapter, we will look at some examples of modern day rune-casting, but this is not exhaustive and the subject is continually evolving, as are the magical interpretations.

Modern Day Rune Casting

Which Runes are right for you?

The runes you choose to buy should feel personal to you. You should wait for a natural inclination towards a type of rune material, style or alphabet. For example, if you are naturally drawn to a specific crystal, then runes carved in that crystal may be right for you.

If you want to feel an even more personal connection to your runes, consider making them yourself. You can simply paint them on pebbles or carve them in wood.

One thought is that the runes are more effective if they are reddened with blood, dye or paint. (Gundarsson, 1990). Please note, the author of this book does not advocate the use of blood in creating a personal set of runes.

The runes do not tell fortunes or predict the future. They provide guidance which can be drawn upon if you choose, and an insight into potential outcomes.

You should decide what you want to gain from reading the runes. When you know this, you will be able to use them in one or more of the following ways.

1. Single Rune Draw

Keep all the runes in a bag or pouch. Clear your mind and think, or even say out loud, the question you wish to ask. It may be about something in the past, present or future. Without looking into the pouch, randomly select one of the runes and place it onto the rune cloth. Next, try to understand the meaning of the rune and how it relates to the question you have asked. It may lead you to your answer or provide an alternative understanding of the subject.

2. Two Rune Draw

With a clear mind, think or say your question and randomly draw two runes from the pouch and place them on the cloth, next to each other.
If the meanings support each other, then they are telling you that something is right and this is supportive. If they oppose each other, then something is wrong and there will be guidance for how to fix it.

3.   Three Norns

As before, ask your question, but this time randomly select three runes and place them next to each other on the cloth.
The far left rune is called the 'Norn Urd'. This gives guidance on the past, relating to your question.
The middle rune is called the 'Norn Skuld'. This gives guidance on the future related to your question.
The far right rune is called the 'Norn Verdandi' and this gives guidance on your question related to the present.

Note, in Norse mythology, the Norns Urd, Skuld and Verdandi are the three females who control fate.

4.   Body, Mind and Spirit

Placing the three runes in this same horizontal line also has an alternative health related reading:
The far left rune represents your current physical condition.
The middle rune represents your current mental condition.
And the far right rune represents your current spiritual condition.
By understanding the meanings of the runes on this context, you can take steps that might help improve your physical, mental and / or spiritual health.

Above: The Norns Urd, Verdandi, and Skuld under the World-tree Yggdrasil" by Ludwig Burger (1882)

Note, in the image above, Norn Skuld has her face partially concealed in a hood, as the future is hidden.

5. Triple Runes

This time, when you randomly select three runes, place them on the cloth in a vertical line. The rune at the bottom gives guidance on your current situation.
The middle rune relates to what you need to do.
The top rune will give you insight as to what will happen as a result of your actions.

6. Four Dwarves

This time, randomly select four runes and place them on the cloth in a diamond shape.

The top rune relates to yours and your ancestors past desires in connection to your question..

The right rune relates to your current desires and feelings around your question.

The left rune refers to the desires and feelings of others in relation to your question.

The bottom rune relates to your innermost secret desires. If the rune is positive, then your desires will succeed within the near future. If it is not positive, then your desire will not be successful.

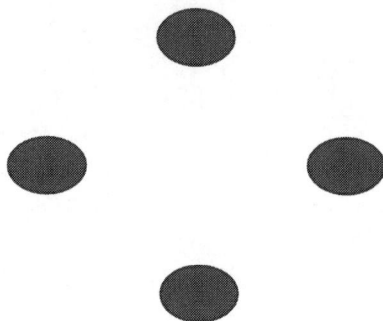

7. Five Rune Formation

Select five random runes from the pouch while thinking or saying your question. Place on the cloth, four in a diamond shape and the fifth in the middle.

The bottom rune relates to what outside influences might affect the question.

The far left rune relates to problems that affect the question.

The top rune relates to positive actions that affect the question.

The far right rune gives guidance towards an answer for the question.

The middle rune relates to how the factors in the question will be influenced in the future.

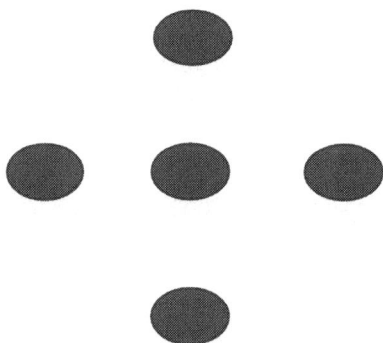

8. Insight Formation

This time, select five runes, and place them in a horizontal line on your cloth.

From left to right, the first rune gives guidance on your present situation.

The second rune gives guidance on the present health of your mind.

The third rune gives guidance on your present heart's desires.

The fourth rune gives guidance on how you currently perceive your life and your plans.

The fifth rune, on the far right, relates to influences that will affect you in the future.

⬬   ⬬   ⬬   ⬬   ⬬

9. Runic Cross Formation

Randomly select six runes while asking your question, and on the cloth, place four in a vertical line and two either side of the second from top rune, making the shape of a cross.

The far left rune gives guidance on past situations.

The middle rune gives guidance on current situations.

The far right rune gives guidance on future situations.

The bottom rune relates to outside influences on your question.

The next rune up gives guidance on what influences are having a positive effect.

The top rune relates to the most likely outcome for the question you have asked.

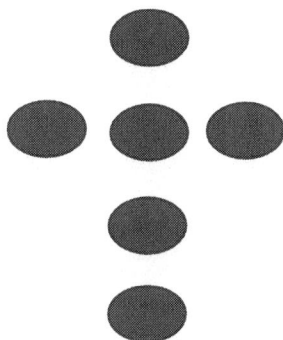

10. Seven Rune Formation

This time, with your question, randomly select seven runes. Place them in a horizontal line, with the middle one lower than the others.

The first and second runes give guidance as to what is the cause of the problem within your question.

The third and fourth runes relate to past influences that have led you into your current situation.

The fifth and sixth runes give you guidance towards understanding and answering your question.

The seventh lowered rune in the middle gives two possible outcomes. If it is positive, then there will be a positive outcome. The outcome will be even more positive if the majority of the other runes are also positive. If the rune is negative, then there will be a negative outcome, and as before, if the majority of the other runes are also negative, then it means the situation will be even more negative.

11. V Formation

Randomly pick seven runes while thinking of your question and place them on the cloth in a V shape.

The top left rune relates to past influences on the question.

The second from top left rune relates to present influences on the question.

The third from top left rune relates to future influences related to the question.

The centre bottom rune gives guidance on the action to take to achieve the best outcome.

The third from top right rune is related to your feelings and emotion regarding the question.

The second from top right rune relates to potential problems regarding the question.

The top right rune offers guidance on the future outcome in relation to the question.

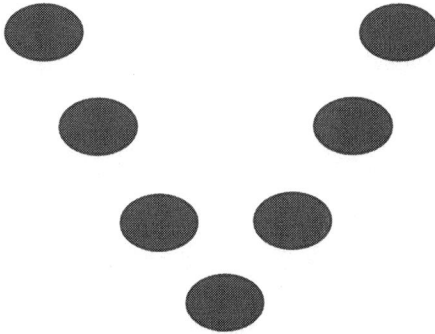

12. Midgard Serpent Formation

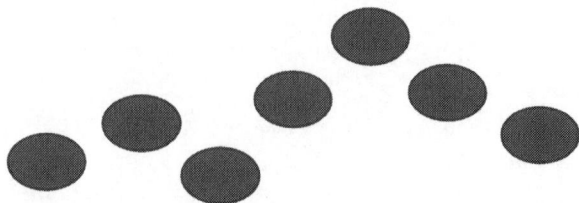

Randomly pick seven runes while thinking of your question and place them on the cloth in a the above serpent shape.

The far left rune is the tail of the serpent and the far right is the head.

Starting from the tail, the far left first rune relates to past feelings about the question.

The next rune relates to our past struggles.

The next rune relates to our current feelings.

The next rune relates to past obstacles that may still be relevant in the present.

The next rune relates to future feelings.

The next rune relates to action to take.

The final far right rune relates to the goal.

13. Bifrost (Bridge) Formation

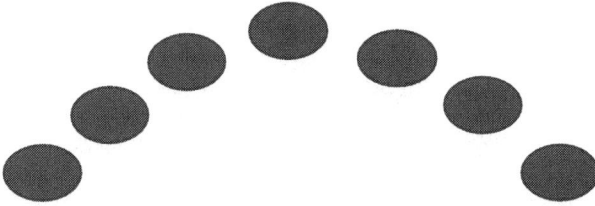

Randomly pick seven runes while thinking of your question and place them on the cloth in a the above bridge shape.

This formation supposedly forms a bridge between the human realm and the divine realm.

It is sometimes referred to as the rainbow formation because of its shape, and colours are designated to each position, from left to right, red, orange, yellow, green, blue, indigo, violet.

From left to right, the far left rune relates to past attitudes.

The next rune relates to the influences of the past.

The next rune relates to current attitudes.

The next rune relates to current influences.

The next rune relates to future attitude.

The next rune relates to future influences.

The last far right rune relates to the outcome.

14. Nine Grid Formation

This time, the runes should be laid on the cloth in three rows of three, each row under the last, thus forming a square shape with a rune in the middle.

The bottom three runes relate to the past. From left to right; the past hidden influences, past known influences, and current feelings about events in the past related to the question.

The centre three runes relate to the present. From left to right; the current hidden influences, the current known influences, and the feelings about the current events related to the question.

The top three runes relate to the future. From left to right; future hidden influences that might adversely affect the outcome, the best possible outcome, and future feelings about the outcome, relating to the question.

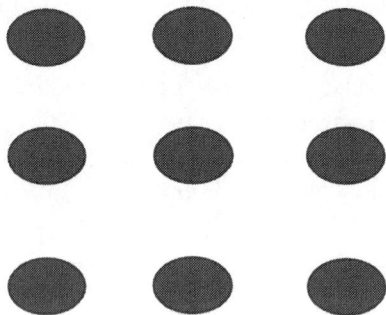

15. Odin's Formation

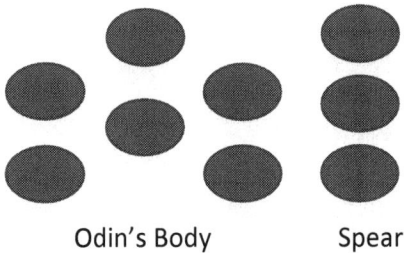

Odin's Body   Spear

Randomly pick nine runes while thinking of your question and place them on the cloth in a the above shape. This shape represents Odin sitting next to his spear.

In Odin's body:

The bottom left rune relates to past influences.

The top left rune relates to past attitudes.

The bottom middle rune relates to current influences.

The top middle rune relates to current attitudes.

The bottom right rune relates to future influences.

The top right rune relates to future attitudes.

In Odin's Spear:

The bottom rune relates to past actions.

The middle rune relates to current actions.

The top rune relates to future actions.

16. Tree of Life Formation

After randomly selecting 10 runes while asking the question, lay them on the cloth in the above formation.

The rune at the top relates to the positive influences on your question.

In the second row, the left rune relates to your physical and mental feelings regarding the question and the right rune relates to your present energy level.

In the third row, .the left rune relates to your current accomplishments with regards to your question and the right rune relates to how morally correct you are in your approach to your question.

The fourth row rune relates to your current health.

In the fifth row, the left rune relates to creative and mindful influences. The right rune relates to love and worries related to the question.

The sixth row rune relates to how your imagination affects your question and the direction your imagination might take you.

The seventh (bottom) row rune gives guidance on current influences in and around your home and home life.

Another formation for the tree of life is:

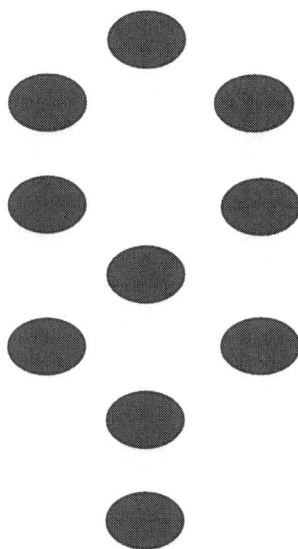

In the above formation, the top central rune is relates to influences.

The top left rune relates to physical and mental health.

The top right rune relates to present energy level.

The second left rune relate to accomplishments.

The second right rune relates to moral code.

The second middle rune relates to present health.

The third left rune relates to matters of the mind.
The third right rune relates to love matters.
The third middle rune relates to imagination and perceived direction.
The middle bottom rune relates to matters at home.

17. Celtic Cross Formation

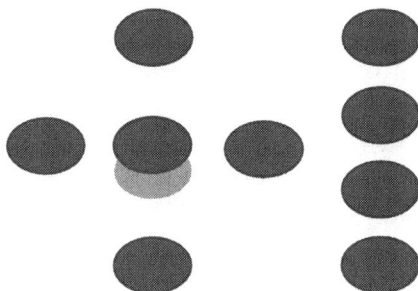

After randomly selecting 10 runes while asking the question, lay them on the cloth in the above cross formation. Note that a couple of runes are stacked in the same position, with one placed upon another. If the shape or your runes do not allow this, then just place them as close to each other as possible, so they are touching.

Beginning with the two stacked runes, the bottom rune relates to the current situation. The top rune relates to future actions that could affect the question.
The far left rune relates to past influences.
In the column of three, the bottom rune relates to current influences. The top rune relates to future influences.
The middle right rune relates to future feelings.
In the column of four, the bottom rune relates to current fears.
The third bottom rune relates to friends and family.
The second top rune relates to beliefs and hopes.
The top rune relates to the future outcome.

18. Egil's Whalebone Formation

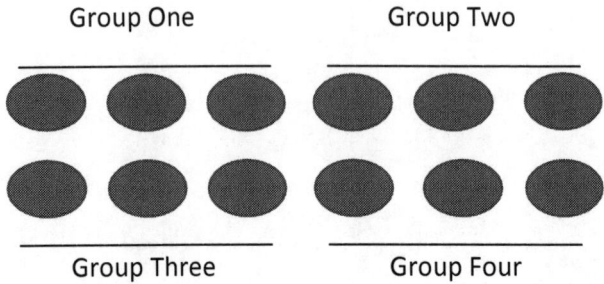

Group One   Group Two

_____   _____

⬤ ⬤ ⬤   ⬤ ⬤ ⬤

⬤ ⬤ ⬤   ⬤ ⬤ ⬤

_____   _____

Group Three   Group Four

After randomly selecting 12 runes while asking the question, lay them on the cloth in the above formation.

Now consider this shape in three groups of four.

Group one relates to your current intentions.

Group two relates to a poor outcome if our intentions are not moral.

Group three relates to concerns and obstacles that influence the goal.

Group four relates to guidance for achieving a good outcome.

19. Full Futhark Formation

The full futhark formation is a reading that is traditionally done on New Year's Day as it provides the answers to questions for the full year ahead.

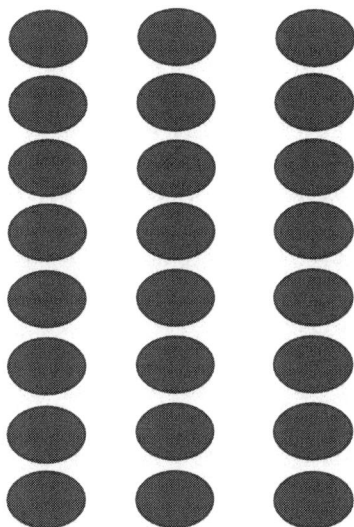

In the left column:
The first (top) rune relates to money and prosperity.
The second rune relates to physical and mental health.
The third rune relates to achieving self-defence or destruction to others.
The fourth rune relates to wisdom and inspiration.
The fifth rune relates to the direction of your life path.
The sixth rune relates to wisdom.

The seventh rune relates to skills you want to master and natural gifts.
The eighth (bottom) rune relates to achieving inner peace and happiness.

In the middle column:
The first (top) rune relates to future life changes.
The second rune relates to your needs to maintain your life path.
The third rune relates to potential obstacles that stand in the way in your life path.
The fourth rune relates to your successes and achievements.
The fifth rune relates to future challenges and decisions to make.
The sixth rune relates to your inner skills.
The seventh rune relates to potential life and death situations.
The eighth (bottom) rune relates to an energy that guides you.

In the right column:
The first (top) rune relates to legal influences and affairs.
The second rune relates to achieving personal growth and natural beauty.
The third rune relates to future friendships and relationships.
The fourth rune relates to your social status.
The fifth rune relates to your emotional health.
The sixth rune relates to sexual influences and emotional encounters.
The seventh rune relates to achieving balance.
The eighth (bottom) rune relates to achieving wealth and wisdom.

Note

An alternative to randomly drawing runes from a pouch or bag, is to pour all the runes out and then, while thinking or verbally asking the question, with your less dominant hand, float your hand over the runes and pick up whichever your hand is drawn to.

Another alternative is to simply pour them all out and randomly pick up the number of runes you require while thinking the question, just whichever your eyes are drawn to. It is difficult to keep a clear mind while using this method though and achieving randomness is tricky.

The key, is to have the runes drawn at random, whichever method you choose.

When you read the runes, having asked your question, you must have your mind remain clear and free to accept any thoughts that are invoked by the guidance you receive from the runes. Simply understand the meaning of the rune that is drawn and apply it to your question. If you are relaxed and your mind is open, then answers will find their way to you.

Remember, how you act on the guidance you receive is up to you. You have freewill, so the choices you make will affect the outcome. Use the runes wisely and they will assist you with your decisions and give you insight into your potential outcomes.

With the use of runes, clarity of mind and steadfast self-belief, you will be able to achieve all that you are hoping for.

References

Barnes, M. P (2012) Runes, A Handbook, Boydell Press

Bernott, K (2019) The Elder Futhark Runes And Their Meanings, shieldmaidenssanctum.com

Birley, A. R. (1999) Agricola and Germany, Oxford World's Classics

Blum, R (1987) The Book of Runes: A Handbook for the Use of an Ancient Oracle, Michael Joseph

Brewer, D (2021) Codes of Alchemy, Lulu Press

British Museum (2017) Collection Search: https://www.britishmuseum.org/collection

Conradt, S (2008) 10 Interesting Runestones, mentalfloss.com

Dalton (1912) Franks Bequest Catalogue of the Finger Rings, BMP, London

Düwel, K. (1983) Runenkunde, 2nd Edition, Stuttgart

Flowers, S. E (2011) Runes and Magic, Lodestar

Groeneveld, E (2018) Runes, worldhistory.org

Gronitz, D (2022) The Rune Site, the runesite.com

Gundarsson, K (aka Grundy, S) (1990) Teutonic Magic, Llewellyn Publications Inc

Jadewik (2012) Björketorp Runestone Curse, 4girlsandaghost.wordpress.com

Koch, J. T (2020) Celto-Germanic, Later Prehistory and Post-Proto-Indo-European Vocabulary in the North and West, University of Wales Centre for Advanced Welsh and Celtic Studies

Krause, W (1971) Die Sprache der Urnordischen Runeninschriften.

Larrington, C (1999) The Poetic Edda, Oxford World's Classics

Levin, J (2010) Alchemy and Economy in Seventeenth Century England.

MacLeod, Mindy & Mees (2006) Runic Amulets and Magic Objects, Woodbridge

Matier, D (2019) Norse Mythology: The Eighteen Charms Known By Odin, discover.hubpages.com

Mees, B (2003) North-Western European Language Evolution

Mesney, P (2017) Anglo-Saxon Runic Rings, Cardiff University

Montelius, O (2010) Sveriges Hednatid, Kessinger Publishing
(Original edition: 1877)

Nationalmuseets Samlinger Online (2017) https://samlinger.natmus.dk

Newcombe, R (unknown) An Introduction to Using the Runes, holisticshop.co.uk

Page, R. I (1987) Runes, Reading the Past, California University Press

Peiper, P (1999) Imitative Kampfesmagie bei den Germanen nach dem Zeugnis von Runeninschriften

Powell, N (1977) Alchemy the Ancient Science, Doubleday

Rives, J. B (2010) Agricola and Germania: Tacitus, Penguin Classics

Schneider, K (1969) Runische Inschriftenzeugnisse zum Stieropferkult der Angelsachsen

Stephens, G (2015) Handbook of the Old-northern Runic Monument of Scandinavia and England, Now First Collected and Deciphered. Sagwan Press
(Original edition: 1866)

Viking Runes and Runestones (2022) historyonthenet.com, Salem Media

Vikingeskibmuseet (unknown) Write as a Viking, www.vikingeskibmuseet.dk

Other Books by D Brewer

If you found this book interesting, you may also like:

Sacred Geometry Book of History, Meanings and How To Create
Them

Shapes and Symbols of Sacred Geometry: A Pocket Reference Book

72 Demon Sigils, Seals and Symbols of the Lesser Key of Solomon:
A Pocket Reference Book

Codes of Alchemy: A Magic Symbol Reference Book

Ancient Celtic Symbols and Their Meanings: A Magic Symbol
Reference Book

Printed in Great Britain
by Amazon

29555965R00090